(how not to do)

A Lap of Ireland

mud, sweat and tears

Richard Georgiou

Email:	richard@onemanonabike.com
website:	www.onemanonabike.com
FaceBook:	Richard Bumpkin Georgiou
Twitter:	@richardgeorgiou
Version:	1.1

ISBN-10: 1516849760
ISBN-13: 978-1516849765

DEDICATION

I dedicate this book to my first dog, George, for simply being there and for patiently listening to me after I failed my first test.

CONTENTS

LESSONS

My first experience of adventure motorcycling was from a single episode of Long Way Down. Not one second after the programme had finished was I on the Internet looking for somewhere to get a motorbike license. I found a place, signed up for an intensive direct access course and entered stage two of my life.

The morning of my first lesson finally arrived and I took a quick look out of the window. It was a freezing cold, soaking wet February morning. This was not going to be a pleasant experience. I raided my chest of drawers and put on almost every item of clothing I had.

I turned up for my first lesson looking like some kind of arctic womble. There were about ten others in the room, all waiting patiently for whatever was going to happen next. I took a seat and waited.

I looked around the room. There were some sexy looking motorbikes at one end, some tools, clothes and the ten of us. Ten people who all had one thing in common. Each and every one of us was knee deep in a mid-life crisis. As I examined each of my fellow wannabe adventure riders in turn I came to the conclusion that I was not some kind of super hero adventurer but just another bloke of a certain age wanting to do something other than the daily routine.

I was sitting there struggling with my new self-appointed label when the door opened and Mr Superbike walked in. He was dressed in a very expensive looking, all in one leather racing suit with a crash helmet under his arm that shouted both money and experience. His boots looked equally as impressive with lots of branding and buckles. Everything was colour coordinated; pristine white was the background with flashes of blue and red for the detail.

The ten of us looked at him with our "we are not worthy" expressions and waited for instruction. Surprisingly, Mr Superbike strutted over to an empty chair and sat down. The room fell silent as we all struggled to believe that he was just one of us.

A few minutes later our instructors arrived; two men and a woman. To my amusement, each of them shot a quick glance at Mr Superbike as they walked through the door. The two men were professional and showed no expression whatsoever but the woman was far more honest, she pulled a face that said 'what the ?' which made me smile.

With introductions done, we were shown upstairs to a classroom where we were taken through the safety stuff and given some waterproofs and a helmet. With more layers than a Spanish onion I struggled with the flattering, day-glow attire but finally managed it and made my way outside to the bikes. This was step one, CBT, or for those unacquainted with the terminology, Compulsory Basic Training.

We were each given a little Honda CB125 and told how to

use it. It really was quite basic stuff. This leaver is called the brake, this is the clutch, et cetera, et cetera. We were then all lined up in a row and told to try starting off. Everyone succeeded with this perfectly with the exception of Mr Superbike who stalled it. He started it up again, revved it violently and stalled it again. I have to admit that I was smiling in my helmet at his misfortune.

One of the instructors helped Mr Superbike with his start off and he finally got rolling, in fact, he really got rolling. He zoomed off, quickly gaining speed and went flying into the fence at the far end. At this point it became apparent that we'd unconsciously split ourselves into two groups; those who could, and those who couldn't.

Our group continued with our start-off and stops and even changed a gear or two and all the time the instructor was trying to educate Mr Superbike with the basics of starting and stopping. Every few minutes there was another crashing noise as gravity and stupidity combined to overcome logic and ability.

After a few hours of starting, stopping, changing gear and going round in circles it was decided that we were ready for the open roads. We were taken out of the station car park and into Haywards Heath. We followed one instructor through the streets and onto the faster roads. I was quite surprised at how vulnerable I felt at 60 mph with cars all around. It was then that I noticed that Mr Superbike was not with us. When we stopped I enquired to his whereabouts.

"Where's Mr Superbike?" I asked.

Kat (my instructor) smiled as she'd not heard his assigned name before.

"Some people just aren't supposed to ride bikes." she said.

It turned out that he'd spent something like £1,300 on some beautiful leathers, helmet and boots to find that he just couldn't ride a bike. After a few hours he admitted defeat and drove home. Poor sod.

With Day One successfully under my belt, I returned home. The drive back was an interesting one. The earlier feelings of vulnerability refused to leave my mind, I found myself driving my car far more carefully than before. I wasn't only learning how to ride a bike, I was learning how to avoid crashes which applied to both riding bikes and driving cars.

When I returned home I talked non-stop to my poor, long suffering wife. I could tell that after about three minutes she switched off her hearing subsystem and just nodded politely every few minutes. I knew this yet I continued. I got the message when I asked her a question.

"So what do you think about Mr Superbike then?" I said.
"Oh yes, absolutely." she said without a pause. It was time to visit the Internet and research bikes.

After a few hours of reading everything I could and looking at what was available I'd narrowed down my choices to a BMW F650GS or a Honda Transalp XL650V. Being a person of limited stature (a short-arse) the other contenders in the dual sport category of motorbike would have left my feet flapping about in the wind. The BMW was going to be easier to ride and had a lower seat but the Honda had two cylinders which meant it would be smoother. It was also tougher and more reliable. My trusty steed would be a Honda Transalp.

I looked through the AutoTrader and found four in my

price range. They were all exactly what I was looking for. Perfect! I sat back and enjoyed the anticipation.

As expected, the following morning brought freezing cold temperatures and drizzle. I got dressed in my womble suit and made my way to Haywards Heath for my next lesson. Today we were going to be introduced to the big bikes.

I tried to listen to the instructors rambling on about safety and stuff but my attention was taken by the bikes in our vicinity. There were two big bike options. A Kawasaki ER6 and a BMW F650GS. I was knee deep in my own little world, riding across the Atlas Mountains to the Sahara when ..

"Richard, what did I just say?" asked Kat rather abrasively. Oh shit.
"Errr .. that it was absolutely vital to pay attention?"

I heard a few chuckles from the others and hoped I'd not made a complete tit of myself. I paid attention to the rest of the briefing and soon enough it was time to get acquainted with the bikes.

We were taken outside and shown our steeds. Being a short arse, I was given one of the BMW's which was fine by me. I looked over at my instructor who told me to take it for a gentle spin around the car park. I got on the bike and .. Oh my God, it was absolutely HUGE! I started off and rode gently around the car park. Not only was this bike huge, it was also incredibly comfortable and very easy to ride. This was not a CB125.

The day was comprised of riding around Haywards Heath and its vicinity. It was fantastic! The bike was super comfortable and had lots of low down grunt. I soon learnt when to use the front brake, when to use the back brake, which foot to put down and to look everywhere all the time. We did some U-turns (which were dead easy on the BMW), hill starts and we even had some lunch which was very welcome.

TEST ONE

Soon enough my test day arrived. To say that I was crapping myself would be a complete understatement. It's not that I'm a nervous kind of chap, it was more about me really wanting to pass. I was introduced to my examiner who seemed like a fun kind of guy, not! I was told that he would be following me in a car and was given an ear piece so I could hear his instruction.

We set off. I did my best to ride well and did lots of looking around. I turned a few corners, went round a few roundabouts and everything seemed to be going okay. Then we hit some traffic. I looked in my mirror but the examiner was gone. It was a novel experience, I was on my test yet the examiner was nowhere to be seen. I continued to follow his instruction for a few minutes then he told me to 'find a safe place to stop, pull over and wait for me.' I did as I was told and waited about 5 minutes for old grumpy bollocks to catch up.

He pulled in behind me and told me that he was going to instruct me to 'do a U-turn when it was safe to do so'. I did my U-turn when it was safe to do so without issue and we continued.

With a few more manoeuvres successfully under my belt it was time to return to the test centre. With one roundabout between me and a completion I thought I was home and dry. I was so adamant that I'd passed that I relaxed. My mind played out the 'Congratulations you've passed' conversation and I was happy!

"Take the first exit at the roundabout." he instructed.

I checked my mirrors and indicated left and continued with my daydream. By the time I arrived at the roundabout I'd completely forgotten where I'd been asked to go and decided it was probably straight over. And that was how I failed my first test.

Going straight over a roundabout whilst indicating left is far from being a minor issue, in fact, if there was someone sitting at that roundabout waiting to go, they'd have seen my indicator and pulled out. I'd then have ridden into their side.

I rode back feeling miserable and humiliated by my own excess of stupidity. We turned up at the training facility and I rebooked my test. The earliest available date at the same place was five weeks away or just two weeks away with the Brighton Marina test centre. I opted for the Marina and waited my two weeks. What a twat!

During the following two weeks I concentrated on keeping my feet firmly on the ground. There were no little trips into my imaginary world, no fantasies about being tall or good looking or bright, just reality. I simply remained in real life. Did you know that some people live their entire lives in reality? I know, it beggars belief.

Having said all that, one good thing did happen in that two week period. I bought a nice Honda Transalp XL650V. It was a 2006 model in dark red with 2,103 miles on the clock. It was in mint condition and arrived in a van. When it turned up we wheeled it out of the van and into my shed. It was even bigger than it was impressive and much higher than the BMW I was used to. I gave the man all my savings (£2000) and paid the remaining £2,200 on my credit card. I didn't start it, I didn't even sit on it. All that could wait until I'd passed my test.

I then visited my local Honda dealer to get kitted out with a helmet and clothes, et cetera. The helmet was simple, the jacket was simple but the trousers were a problem. If I got the right length the waist was too small. If I got the right waist the legs were too long. I enquired if they had anything for short and fat people but it seemed not. I thought I was very clever by selecting a size somewhere in between the two; however, what it actually meant was the waist was too small *and* the legs were too long. £700 later I was back at home with my biker garb. Please, please, please let me pass my test.

I looked up the test routes on the Internet and my wife and I drove around them in the car. There was an element of me which felt it was cheating but I really wanted to pass and if that meant cheating, then so be it. There didn't seem to be any particularly difficult bits but I think just knowing that I was familiar with all the possible routes helped my nerves considerably.

TEST TWO

The day of my second test came round soon enough and I was feeling confident. My instructor Kat and I rode to the test centre in the Brighton Marina. When we found out who my examiner was, Kat let out a deep sigh.

"He's a tough one. Good luck!"

She gave me a manly pat on the back and told me I'd be fine. The examiner followed me in his car and gave instruction through my ear piece. I was desperate to pass but, for some reason, I didn't feel as nervous as the first time. The test went well and before I knew it I was back in the office with the examiner.

"Well, I'm pleased to tell you that you have passed."

I just about managed to stop myself from grabbing the man and placing a giant smacker on the top of his bald head. I smiled politely and said thank you. After signing a few forms, and with a skip in my step, I left the building.

Outside, Kat was waiting for me and my news. I waved my

pieces of paper and grinned like an idiot. Smiling, she took the forms and looked over them. I had a clean pass! It wasn't often someone got a clean sheet and even less often with the examiner that I had. Perhaps I'd made up for my dismal failure in my last test. Now the fun could begin.

The ride back to Haywards Heath was fantastic. Kat's riding style changed completely and I got my first inkling of her experience and ability. I watched in awe as she swooped around bends with an elegance I could only dream of. It didn't take long to get back. When we arrived at the training centre I put my BMW inside and made my way to the kitchen for a coffee. We talked about various things like not going out in jeans and a tee-shirt, like how showing-off can end in humiliation and about how motorbikes actually kill people.

One of the things Kat told me was that it's bad to be the meat in a car sandwich. She told me that if you have to stop behind a car and there's a possibility of being hit from behind, to always position your bike at an angle so you can make a quick escape if necessary. Three years later this very fact saved my life as I rode into Tangier. For that, I will always be in her debt.

I got home and told my wife Flowie my news. Flowie was happy for me and gave me a congratulations card with a picture of a black cat on the front. I felt tired but most of all relieved. After a shower I went out to my shed and sat on my bike. My word, it really was very different to the BMW. The seat was far higher, it felt top heavy but it was also built like a tank. This was to be the beginning of a long life of adventure we were to have together. I started it up and listened to it ticking over. It was my bike and I had a license to ride it. I was one happy bunny.

The following day I arranged tax and insurance and took it

out for a ride. The first 300 yards were up a dirt track to the main road. My first impressions were of how different it felt to the BMW. It was much higher and more unstable at slow speeds; however, the engine was far smoother and it had an air of immense toughness about it. This was a bike that could take everything it was given and still come back for more.

Once I got onto the main road the difference between the single cylinder engine of the BMW and the twin in my Transalp really started to show. It felt quicker, more responsive and far smoother. Everything about it said quality. I was very happy with my purchase.

Over the following few months I took the bike out for various Sunday morning rides and small trips. After one ride I got home and was trying to get my trusty steed back into my shed when I lost my balance and dropped it. I just about managed to pick it up but remember being astounded by how heavy it was. Upon checking the bike over I found that I'd broken the front brake lever and smashed the right hand mirror. These were duly ordered from the Honda dealer and fitted two days later by me in my driveway. As I was pushing the bike back into the shed I dropped the bloody thing again. I checked the bike over and found that I'd broken the front brake lever and smashed the right hand mirror, again.

I didn't mind buying another mirror and lever, however with my inexperience, short height and stupidity level, this could get tiresome. I decided what I needed was to make it *Georgiou proof*. I did some Internet surfing and found a company called Acerbis who make hand guards. I bought their best ones and fitted them to the bike. I then pushed the bike over to see what snapped off. Absolutely nothing!

FANCY A TRIP TO IRELAND?

The weather soon started to warm up as we entered spring and thoughts of a little adventure started bouncing around in my head. Time ticked on, work took over for a while and before I knew it summer was upon us. And all the time, there in the background, the feeling of wanting a little adventure was getting stronger and stronger. Then one evening my wife and I were invited to a mate's birthday party. His name was Steve.

We turned up and did the party thing. We drank alcohol, ate too much food and had a great time. We did the rounds and met lots of nice people. Later on that evening Steve told me that he had a business meeting in Ireland and was going to zip up there on his BMW R1200GS and asked if I would like to come. He'd do the meeting and I'd ride around Ireland. Oh yes!

I had two weeks to get myself ready. Upon getting home I went straight on the Internet and bought two aluminium panniers and a mounting frame. They had to be shipped from Germany so delivery was going to take 7 to 10 days. I already had loads of camping stuff so I just had to hope that my panniers would arrive in time.

Over the next week I worked out exactly what I needed to take. The panniers I'd bought were pretty big and my North Face duffle bag was huge so I had loads of space to fill with camping stuff and goodies. I drew up my inventory.

After a few panicked emails to Touratech I'd pretty much given up hope of the panniers turning up before I left but at 8:30 on the evening before I was due to leave, they finally arrived.

After a few hours (and the biggest blood blister you've ever seen) I had them fitted and they looked good. Actually, what they really looked was big but I liked them. I spent most of the night filling them with all the *essentials* of a motorbike camping trip. I had all the camping stuff plus a good range of tinned foods, some coffee, a fine selection of English and French cheeses, a nice bottle of red and one of white. I checked my watch as I got into bed, it was 4:15. I set my alarm for 6:30 and closed my eyes.

TIME TO LEAVE

The next thing I knew the alarm was going off. I lay there for a few moments wondering who I was until lucidity arrived. Aaaaah, I was Richard Georgiou, I passed my motorbike test and I'm going on an adventure! I clambered out of bed and made my way downstairs to the kitchen. I managed to put the kettle on without breaking anything, made myself a strong black coffee and sat down. I was very tired.

The coffee woke me up a little and soon enough it was time to get the bike out of the shed. I opened the back doors and wheeled it out. Christ it was heavy! I thought about dumping a few tins of chilli con carne or perhaps the wine or fine cheeses but what was camping without chilli, wine or cheese? I decided to just man up and deal with the weight. I put my gear on and bounced up my lane to the main road. The bike did feel heavy but once underway it wasn't too bad.

The ferry was booked for 2:30 in the afternoon but we had to ride to Fishguard in south Wales to catch it so had arranged to meet early at a place just outside of East

Grinstead. I rode to our meeting place with the excitement of anticipation. On the way there I thought about the plan for the first day.

Steve and I would meet up and ride to Fishguard together. We'd then jump on the ferry to Rosslare and spend the three and a half hours eating and sleeping. When we arrived at Rosslare at 6pm fully refreshed Steve would head north to his business meeting and I'd head west and begin my lap around Ireland. My first aim would be to find a nice camp site. I'd then spend the evening staring at the beautiful Irish countryside watching the sun go down as I enjoyed my chilli con carne, fine cheeses and wine. That was my plan for the first day. What could go wrong?

I met up with Steve, we said our hellos and set off. We zipped along quickly eating up the miles, at around the half way point we ran into a long traffic jam but managed to just about squeeze our panniers through the gaps and continued onwards. As we got closer to Wales the sky started to cloud up a little but it was still mostly sunny. We stopped for fuel and coffee then made our way through Wales until we reached Fishguard. I've never been that great at working out ports and usually end up getting told off for going wrong but luckily I was following Steve, and Steve was an expert! Soon enough we were in the queue for the ferry. We left the bikes and went off for some food.

When it was time to board the ferry we returned to our bikes and rode to the front of the queue. The push bikes went first, and then it was us. I carefully rode onto the metal ramp and into the ferry. We were asked to turn the bikes around and to put the front wheels into the slots. Steve managed to get his huge GS in no problem but I was finding it all a bit much. I jumped off the bike and attempted to man handle it but almost dropped it. It really was bloody heavy! I muttered something about my fine selection of English and French cheeses being incredibly heavy but no one noticed. Steve came to the rescue and helped and finally it was done. We locked 'em up and made our way upstairs for some food and relaxing.

We found some seats, dumped our stuff and waited for the restaurant to open. We sat there talking easily about life and bikes and stuff. It was nice just sitting there with my friend talking. After a few huge metal against metal clonks that resonated around the entire ferry, we set off. Steve and I made our way to the restaurant and ordered our food. As we sat there eating and talking I noticed that the sky was getting darker.

WE ARRIVE IN IRELAND

When the ferry docked in Rosslare I looked outside to see that the sky had grown even darker still. We rode off the ferry with the dread that every biker feels just before a downpour. We pulled over, wished each other good luck and went our separate ways. Steve went north for his meeting and I went west towards the dark, ominous clouds.

A few minutes later the heavens opened. To simply use the word *rain* would not do the phenomenon justice; it was like being at the bottom of a waterfall. I did my best to continue riding but the view through my visor had all but disappeared. I struggled on until I saw a few large trees overhanging the road. I pulled over and stopped. The trees afforded me a little protection from the wind and rain but not a great deal. I was still getting wet and I was still miserable. With my visor completely misted up I removed my helmet. Not two seconds after it had slid off the top of my head, a van flew right through the large puddle I was next to and completely covered me in dirty water and grit. This was not the motorcycle nirvana I had imagined.

After twenty minutes or so the rain started to ease. I needed to find some kind of camp site so clambered back aboard the bike and continued. It was a miserable ride, the temperature had dropped, it was starting to get dark and the rain continued to fall. After about half an hour of riding through the rain I found what I was looking for, kind of. It was a sign post and on it was a picture of a small tent. I turned left and followed the sign down a small track that turned into a seriously boggy field full of cow shit. The far end was higher and overhung by trees so I decided, in my infinite wisdom, to ride through the field to the top.

If I was on a motocross bike with gnarly off-road tyres I'm quite sure it would have been easy; however, I was not on a motocross bike, and I didn't have gnarly off-road tyres. Instead, I was on a heavily loaded up Honda Transalp with road tyres and as such, it was far from easy, in fact it would be fair to say, it was damn right messy!

I rode onto the field and instantly felt the bike slip. I stood up on the pegs and gripped the tank with my knees as I changed into second gear. Keeping the revs low I slowly chugged up the field to the far end. Whilst revelling in my success and manliness I opened the throttle. The back end slid about but I just about managed to keep control. I'm not sure what the collective noun is for *cowpat*, but suffice to say there were lots of them. As I rode up the steepest part the back wheel spun causing large quantities of cow shit to be ejected in all directions. But it didn't matter, because I was upright and I was at the top of the field. I had made it.

I stood there next to the bike with a huge grin from the adrenalin that was still surging through my veins. I could clearly see my route up the field, there was a wiggly and deep groove up the middle surrounded by ample splatters of cow *ejecta* on both sides. The bike had a healthy coating too but I have to admit, it did look most impressive sitting there dripping in excrement!

I found the driest spot which was under some trees and moved the bike closer. The tent was unpacked and set up, as were my pink, blow-up camping mattress and ex-army sleeping bag. The wind had really whipped up and the temperature had dropped significantly which meant more serious rain. I hurried around getting ready for my evening feast. One bottle of Merlot, a small selection of fine cheeses and a tin of chilli con carne were removed from my left pannier. A tin opener, some coffee, a pot, a tin cup, a bottle of water and my petrol stove were removed from the right.

I retreated to the tent, set up my stove in the porch and attempted to light it. Now, at this point I would like to point out that I love my stove. It's made by Coleman, it burns petrol and I've had it for years. It's a little like me I suppose, it's not the quickest, or the quietest, you could even say it's somewhat temperamental; however, it always gets there in the end. Lighting it is something that needs to be done with confidence, be a man and just light it and all is fine, let it know you're scared and it'll blow your fingers off.

I pumped the pusher on the side thirty times, turned the knob to high and lit a match. I confidently waved the match over the top and WOOF! The stove was alight.

After extinguishing my once hairy arms I placed my pot of water on the stove and sat back with the contentment of a job well done.

I took the small LED lantern that I keep in my tent and hung it on a tree branch about twenty feet away to keep the mosquitoes away. I drank my coffee as the last of the light disappeared and the rain poured down.

The chilli con carne was well below par which was somewhat disappointing; however, this was more than offset by the splendour of my fine selection of English and French cheeses. And when combined with a nice glass or three of Merlot made for a most pleasant evening.

The rain persisted as I munched my way through the *Camembert*, the rather stinky *Stinking Bishop* and even the rather hard going, and incredibly pongy, *Pont L'Eveque*.

The wine flowed as the cheese slipped down and before I knew it I was looking around to see who'd drunk the last half of the Merlot. When I attempted to move my body to the wooded area for a pee I realised that it was most certainly me. As much as I'd love to tell you how I successfully made it to the wooded area and back safely, the truth is that I can't actually remember. All I know is that I woke up with a cracking headache and covered in cow shit.

DAY TWO

In my mind I pictured the mornings of a motorbike camping trip to be full of things like anticipation for the ride ahead, enjoying the sunrise whilst drinking a nice cup of strong coffee, happy faces and happy people. The only similarity that my morning had with this was that it was in fact, morning.

I had a cracking headache, my trousers and boots were covered in shit and I had to literally peel my tongue from the roof of my mouth in order to swallow. I gently exited the tent into the pouring rain and squelched my way to the bike. I found some paracetamol and ibuprofen and managed to make it back to the tent without falling over. I climbed in and took my tablets.

Every move of my head hurt, I needed coffee. I'd left my stove out in the rain all night and it was full of water but I had faith. I shook the water off and pumped it until it felt like my head was about to burst open. I turned the knob to high, lit a match and waved it over the hob. The warmth from the temporary fireball felt wonderful, but all too soon it was replaced by the misery of reality and the smell of burning hair. I put the water on the stove and waited for it to boil.

As I sat there consumed by misery, I thought about how much I wanted a cigarette. I'd finally taken the plunge and packed up about six months ago. It had been quite a battle but one I felt I'd won because the cravings had gone. Nope, I was stronger than that.

I tipped the boiling water into my cup and made myself a coffee. After ten minutes, the tablets and coffee started taking effect but I still felt crap. What I needed was food. The rain was still coming down as hard as ever but it looked like a break was slowly heading in my direction. I broke out a tin of baked beans and sausages and stuck it on the stove. It was just what I needed, which was lucky because the only alternative was some left over *Pont L'Eveque* and I wasn't confident that I'd be able to keep such a substance down.

I started to feel better after the beans. The sky got a little lighter, the rain slowed to a drizzle and I found an exit from the field that didn't include cow shit. All of a sudden life wasn't looking so bad.

I spent the next half an hour packing everything back onto the bike. The rain stopped as I got ready to depart and I found myself actually looking forward to the days riding. My first stop was to find a petrol station so I could jet wash the bike.

Getting out of the field wasn't quite as straight forward as I'd hoped. The overnight rain had brought the ground to saturation point and as I attempted to ride over the last part the front wheel slipped and I dropped the bike. I was going slowly so no harm was done to anything but my pride. I was happy to see that my mirror and brake lever remained intact. Surprisingly, picking the bike up wasn't as bad as I had imagined and I had it upright again in no time. I carefully rode onto the road and continued west until I found a petrol station.

I pulled in and asked for a token for their jet wash. The girl behind the counter looked at me, then over at the bike. She smiled and gave me an extra token.

"One for your bike and one for you gorgeous." She said in her beautiful southern Irish accent.

I thanked her and left hoping she hadn't noticed my red face. I pushed the bike over to the jet wash, put my token in the slot and took hold of the lance. I gave my bike and luggage a damn good blasting until everything was pretty much dirt free. I glanced over at the checkout as I used my second token to blast myself clean. Ms Checkout was sitting there on her stool staring right at me. When she saw me looking over she waved and gave me a big smile. I smiled back, stuck my crash helmet on and buggered off. Blimey, that's not happened for a while! I felt embarrassed but also quite chuffed. I smiled as I covered the next twenty miles.

I'd not covered much distance the previous day so I was quite keen to get some miles under my belt. I decided to stick to the coast road as much as I could so set my target for Clonakilty in the southwest. It was about 140 miles away but more on the wiggly coast roads. I thought that if I could get there, I would then head inland until I found a nice place to camp. Hopefully a nice clean field free from cattle and their aftermath!

As I wound my way through the wonderful lanes of southern Ireland the clouds slowly dispersed and the sky turned blue. The temperature settled in the mid-twenties and, with a beautiful vista around each corner, I felt I had entered motorcycle nirvana. If it stayed like this tonight's camping was going to be fantastic.

About half way there I passed a small shop and decided to stop and buy some provisions for the night's camping. Stuff the tinned rubbish, I wanted some proper sustenance. I bought some freshly made butchers sausages, some free range eggs, a pack of streaky bacon, some black pudding and some salted butter. I also bought a large coffee and walnut cake for lunch.

As I continued on meandering through the beautiful lanes, I noticed that the sky was almost cloudless. I stopped at the side of the road next to a fabulous view of hills and lakes, sat on a wall and enjoyed my cake. It was divine! It was moments like these that made the not so lovely moments bearable. The memory of hacking through piles of sodden cow shit seemed like a thousand lifetimes away; however, the memory of Ms Checkout smiling at me seemed only a few minutes back.

I finished my cake and checked the map. I was heading in a south-westerly direction and was doing okay. It was taking longer than expected because of the little winding lanes but that didn't matter. I had time and couldn't think of a better way to spend it than swooping around the awe-inspiring roads of Ireland.

The afternoon was beautiful, the sun shone down, the roads were idyllic, the birds twittered away at full volume and, on top of all that, approaching was an evening of exquisite <biker> food and white wine aplenty.

I reached my destination and bumbled around for a while looking for a nice place to pitch my tent. I rode down lots of little lanes and ended up a few clicks south of a place called Glangarrif. I turned onto a tiny track then spotted a super place to camp for the night. It meant riding over a few hundred yards of rough ground but I took it easy and made it without a problem.

It was the perfect camp site. It was secluded, beautiful and quiet and to top it all off, it had an uninterrupted view of the North Atlantic Ocean. I parked the bike and unpacked everything. The tent was up and facing the sea inside of five minutes and ten minutes after that everything was ready for my idyllic evening. I made myself a coffee and just enjoyed my surroundings as the birds sung and the butterflies fluttered around in the breeze.

I finished my coffee and soon enough I'd opened the white. As I sat there sipping my Chardonnay in my little corner of heaven I thought about all the elements that had come together to allow me to be there. I was thinking about my motorbike, passing my test, my job, et cetera, when it came to me. All that I was really missing before all that was the *idea*. People travel all over the world on nothing but a moped. My flashy bike just made it a bit faster and a little more comfortable.

As I continued thinking about life and such things I set up my stove and cooking pot. A dollop of butter went in first, then the sausages, and ten minutes later the black pudding. My baked beans were cooking away in their own tin and five minutes later it was all done. I dished it up as I cooked the bacon and fried the eggs. I forced myself not to pick at the black pudding or sausages but instead, to wait until everything was ready. It smelt fantastic and soon enough the bacon and eggs were ready too and added to my plate. Wow, what a feast.

When a long hard day meets an old style fry up the result can only be described as mouth-wateringly wonderful.

With dinner complete I found a nice spot to sit, drank my wine and watched the sun disappear over the horizon. I think it would be fair to say that I'd had a good day.

After my dinner I climbed into the tent, got comfy and spent the next two hours reading. I slipped off to sleep.

I awoke to a most alarming thump. It was pitch black and I was in the middle of a gale. I could hear the wind howling as it blew through the trees above me. I felt around for my lantern but couldn't find it. The brief illumination from a flash of lightening allowed me to spot it and I exited the tent. I didn't have to search for long to see what had rudely awoken me from my slumber; a tree had come down not ten feet from my bike. Christ I was lucky!

Seeing the downed tree and listening to the wind howling put me on edge. I stumbled and tripped my way to a clearing and stood there wondering what I was going to do next when the first few hail stones came down. Within ten seconds all hell was breaking lose, the sky was alive with lightening and the hail came down with a force that ripped leaves off the trees. I quickly retreated back to the tent. I checked the tent over but all was fine, it was still standing and there were no leaks.

The thunder and lightning went on for a few hours but the hail turned to rain after a few minutes. It was going to be another messy ride trying to get out of this place in the morning. I tried to sleep but each time I got close to dropping off I'd be awoken by either a clap of thunder or the wind howling through the trees. I eventually dropped off and slept like a log. When I woke I looked at my watch, it was half past ten!

DAY THREE

I'd missed my early start so taking time to make myself a nice coffee wasn't really going to make any difference. It was still raining and windy, which meant I had a day of misery to look forward to. I opened my tent and took a look outside. The daylight brought home the size of the tree that had come down. It was big and it had completely blocked my exit to the road. I stood there for some time thinking about how terribly it could have ended.

I looked around to see how I was going to get the bike out but nothing obvious jumped out at me. Moving the tree was definitely out of the question so I had no choice, I was going to have to push my way through the wooded area and try not to get stuck.

I made myself a coffee and thought about my exit. I refused to believe there wasn't a better way but decided to deal with that when I had to. As I drunk my coffee in the tent I couldn't help but feel the presence of an impending disaster. I told myself to be positive but when did that ever help? There was one thing for it. I finished my coffee and packed everything onto the bike.

I walked around the area to find the best exit but found that my options were seriously limited. I made my decision but it was not going to be pretty. First I was going to have to push my way through about thirty feet of serious undergrowth, then I'd drop down into a small stream and follow that for about twenty feet. The stream looked like the easy part, it was exiting the stream that was going to be tricky as it was muddy and wet. Not a good combination for a bloody heavy bike!

I thought about leaving some of the bags off the bike but the panniers would have to be pretty much emptied to be removed so decided to just give it a go with it fully loaded up. I stood there shaking my head thinking *This is just never going to work*. The bike was already pointing in the right direction so I climbed aboard and slowly made my way to the entrance of the undergrowth. At first I edged my way forward but after a few feet I just stood up on the pegs and went for it. To my astonishment the bike barged its way through perfectly and soon enough I was at the stream, I rode down a small decline into the stream which was okay too. My heart skipped a beat when the front wheel sunk into the silt but they're big wheels and I was able to keep everything moving.

About ten feet later I got stuck. I tried again but with every rotation of the wheel it sunk a little more. I got off the bike and checked out my situation. It was not good, the front wheel was pretty much up to the axle and the back wheel was in over the axle. I wobbled it and wiggled it but nothing seemed to make any difference. When I'd read about other people getting stuck, or seen them on TV I always thought that they should simply push the bike over onto its side and drag it out one wheel at a time. This was my plan.

I switched the bike off, wobbled it left and right a few times to loosen it up, and then pushed it over. I grabbed the back wheel and slid the bike over to the bank and did the same with the front. Now all I had to do was to stand it up again. My normal method was to turn my back on the bike, put my backside against the seat and use my legs to lift but because of the bank this was not an option. After half an hour of trying to lift the bike up I came to the conclusion that it was not going to happen. I was knackered, cold and seriously miserable.

I grabbed the back wheel and slid the bike over to the other side of the stream and did the same for the front. I was now able to lift the bike up using my normal method. Thirty seconds later the bike was upright again.

"Please, please, please start my beloved baby."

I pressed the starter button; it turned over twice then jumped into life. *Thank you!* I edged forward until I reached the place where I was to exit the stream. If I could get the bike out here it would be a short ride over a muddy field to the road. As the front wheel hit the incline the weight of the bike just pushed it deep into the bank, there was just no way it was getting up there. I stopped the bike and thought for a moment. I figured that if I could spread the weight of the bike over a larger area it might not sink and perhaps I'd be able to get the bloody thing out of the stream. I found a few small branches and placed them sideways over the bank. It looked like it might actually work which gave me hope so I found some more and after half an hour or so I'd built up a little ramp. It looked good but whether it would work was anyone's guess. I didn't hang around I just went for it. The front wheel went up nicely and to my surprise I kept on going. I'd made it!

I bounced and bumped my way over the field feeling completely elated and a little shocked. When I spotted the road I attempted to change direction but had entered a boggy area and lost control. I was so knackered that I just sat on my seat and let the bike take me down. My feet remained on the pegs and my hands on the grips even though the bike and I were lying on our side. I squirmed around in the cold mud and managed to get my leg free.

"Shit!" I exclaimed.

I tried to pick the bike up but the ground was so slippery that I ended up sitting back in the mud. I wondered if this was the end of the trip, perhaps I should cut the trip short and just ride home?

After a few minutes I managed to get the bike upright again, I glanced briefly at my mud encrusted bike, got on and rode onto the road. Once the bike was on the road I went back for my helmet. I was very conscious of the fact that when I rode off the bike was going to throw large clods of mud everywhere.

I was about to get on the bike when I spotted a dog walker walking towards me. *Here we go* I thought. She looked at me and slowed as she got closer.

".. and I do this for *pleasure!*" I said with a big smile.

The look on the lady's face made it quite clear that she didn't approve one iota. It was time to make haste and if the lady got covered in large clods of soggy mud then so be it. I put my helmet on and rode off.

It was so nice to be back on a road doing a reasonable speed again. The sky was heavy and it looked like rain was imminent but however hard it was going to be, it was not going to be hard enough to get me or the bike cleaned up. What I needed was another jet wash. Once I was clean I was going to stick to the tarmac!

I rode into a small petrol station with a jet wash machine at the far end. To my surprise it took pound coins and not tokens. I stumbled around in my pocket and found a couple of quid. Over the next twenty minutes I cleaned the bike, my crash helmet, my jacket and my trousers. I moved the bike into a parking space and went inside for a well-deserved, and much needed coffee.

I bought my coffee and was about to climb aboard one of their stalls when I noticed that I was leaving a trail of dirty water behind me, everyone else had noticed too. I apologised, changed direction and took my coffee outside into the pouring rain.

I sipped my coffee as I stood there trying hard not to hate Ireland and its miserable weather. The people in the petrol station looked nice and warm and dry but I was a bit of a mess and I could understand them not wanting me inside. I could see a few people moving things around inside but to be honest, I was too busy trying not to spill my coffee from the sporadic violent shivering episodes to notice.

Just then the door slid open and man came out and told me that they'd got a table and chair for me inside. He handed me a towel and directed me towards the chair. I sat there in awe of the kindness of the human race. It wasn't just the random kindness of one man, a whole group of people helped. I was given another coffee and a warm Cornish pasty. I sat there for about half an hour slowly drying out and warming up.

I paid my bill and walked out into a brief, and rare, moment of glorious sunshine. I climbed aboard my bike and headed for Castlemaine. I was quite keen on sticking to the coastline looking out at nothing but the Atlantic Ocean, with nothing between myself and America.

Castlemaine was where I could turn left and head towards the most western point of Ireland.

As I made my way north the sky grew darker and darker. I could see the rain pouring down up ahead so decided to stop before I got completely soaked and put on my waterproofs. I pulled over in a layby at the side of the road. Now, I would like to say at this point that I've never got on with waterproofs.

<rant> I hate the rustling noise they make, I can never get the bloody things on because of the stupid diagonal zip and I just hate them. Also, why should I spend £700 on waterproof motorbike clobber if I've then got to put waterproofs over the top of them when it rains? Perhaps when I was a baby I was forced to wear rubbers for longer than was absolutely necessary. <rant over>

Having just said all that, I was starting to warm up and dry out so the waterproofs were deemed a necessary evil. I removed them from my bag and shook them out. I unzipped the completely stupid diagonal zip and tried to work out which hole was which.

As the rain edged closer I decided to just go for it. I put my left foot through the large hole thinking that feet are larger than hands. I then looked for the hole for my right foot but there didn't seem to be one. Not believing that even I was stupid enough to purchase the amputee version by mistake I continued. I stumbled around as the rain started to fall and stuffed my right foot into another hole. I pulled the rest up but I'd definitely gone wrong somewhere. Not allowing myself to be beaten by a £20 piece of shitty plastic I tried to put my left arm into the only hole available. This was just not working. I removed it and started again.

"Okay, you're a grown man Mr Georgiou. You can do this."

By this time the rain was really coming down and the layby was fast becoming a pond but I refused to be beaten. I put both my feet into the only holes that could accommodate them. I then pulled the rest up and managed to get one of my arms in. I tried zipping the stupid zip up but needed to pull the material closer together before I could. I struggled and struggled getting more pissed off by the minute. At one point it seemed I'd turned the waterproofs into a giant funnel, water was being directed into the left pocket of my jacket, then into my trousers. This was when I lost my temper.

"Will you give me a fucking break!" I exclaimed as I used every muscle in my body to yank the top up further. This did not have the desired effect. Instead it forced my legs backwards and threw me to the ground. I landed in the sodden layby facedown which pissed me off even more. I tried to get one of my arms out but it was trapped by the suit. I kicked my legs but that just pulled my arms back further. I was in the midst of a God almighty paddy when a car entered the layby and skidded to a stop right next to me.

"Are you alright? Are you alright?" the lady shouted with a look of sheer panic on her face.

"I'm fine! Just get me out of this fucking suit!" I shouted.

She managed to roll me over onto my back and sit me up. From there, between the two of us, we managed to peel my soaked and filthy body out of the waterproofs.

I thanked her and squelched my way back to the bike

muttering something about how I would "rather fucking drown than be strangled to death by a plastic fucking suit". I was not happy.

The suit was duly jumped on and thrown into the nearest bin. Ms Charity drove off with a smile on her face and a dinner table story that would last her for years to come. There's never a dull moment on a Georgiou adventure!

I got back on the bike and headed north into the rain. It was absolutely hammering down but I didn't care, I was just happy to be out of that suit.

After an hour of being rained on and a detour which took me in a nice thirty mile circle I decided that it was time to wimp out and find somewhere nice to stay. I saw a pub, pulled over and stopped. I shook as much water and dirt off my jacket as I could and spent some time wiping my feet. I walked over to the bar and asked for a Guinness, it seemed the right thing to do.

"We don't serve Guinness here." I looked at the chap but couldn't tell whether he didn't want to serve me because I was a soggy wet biker or if he was actually telling the truth.

"Well, perhaps a pint of Murphys then."

He looked back and shook his head. I took a few moments to think about my situation. I could allow myself to be walked over and just leave or I could kick up a stink and end up getting my head kicked in.

"Listen, friend. I've had a shit day, In fact, I've had a shit couple of days and to be quite honest, I'm not really in the mood to put up with any more shit. Now, I considerately shook the water from my jacket outside, I carefully wiped me feet as I entered and I've been nothing but polite. Here's my money, where's my drink?"

He smiled, put his hand on my shoulder and told me I had balls. He got my money and I got my Guinness. The evening went well after that and I seemed to be the centre of attention. At about nine the barman asked if I needed a place to stay. I told him that I wanted somewhere dry, warm and with a bath. To my surprise the pub had its own little cottage next door. Perfect.
I unpacked my bags from the bike and made my way to the cottage. On the way I passed the barman.

"Where you heading?"
"North." I said.
"What, over the border?"
"Yep, and then Scotland."
"Be careful up there. They're not nice like us southerners." I smiled and went to my cottage.

I unlocked my door and made my way inside. Wow, it was beautiful and exactly what I needed. It had a cosy living room with a sofa in front of the TV, the kitchen was good, the bedroom comfy and the bathroom had a double sink, a bath and lots of candles.

I had a wonderful bath then spent the next hour using their hair dryer to dry out my jacket and trousers. I made myself a potent coffee and then slipped into the most comfortable bed in the entire history of beds and the Universe. I closed my eyes and even before I got a chance to do the *crikey I'm so comfy* smile, I was sound asleep.

I slept solidly for about twenty minutes at which point my body decided it had had enough sleep and was ready to start a new day. I tossed and turned, watched some TV, tried to sleep again, watched a film, then just lay on the bed staring at the ceiling. I just wasn't tired. I got up, had a shower and made myself a coffee. I looked at the map and worked out my route to our agreed meeting place, it was 230 miles away which was quite a distance considering the windy Irish roads but easily doable. We'd agreed to meet up close to the border in a place called Sligo. From there we'd have some dinner then head to Belfast where we'd find somewhere to stay.

DAY FOUR

Before I left I went back to the pub for some breakfast; boiled eggs and soldiers with a wonderful cup of strong, fresh coffee. When I finished I attempted to pay for my room and breakfast but was told that it was all on the house by order of the management! Crikey, I left a large tip and got underway.

Even though I'd had almost no sleep and was incredibly tired, the ride to Sligo was nice. My groin was completely dry which was a wonderful novelty and the rain held off for most of the journey.

I finally rode into Sligo at around five. Steve was standing there beside his huge BMW, I rode up and stopped. We did the meet and greet thing and I followed Steve to a restaurant he knew of.

We talked as we ate. Steve told me that his meeting had gone well and I told Steve about my antics. I think Steve was just as dumbfounded as I was about my weird journey but it gave us both a good laugh. There's nowt quite as funny as someone else's misfortune!

The plan for the evening was to ride into Northern Ireland and to visit the house where Steve lived as a kid.

"It's not the kind of place where you'd want to stop" he said "we'll just ride through, quickly." I kind of assumed he was joking but you could feel the tension in the air. Union flags on one side of the road and the Republic of Ireland tricolour flags on the other. Steve wasn't kidding when he said we wouldn't be stopping. I just about saw Steve point to a small terraced house as we zoomed through, it must have been his childhood home. Crikey.

We rode around Northern Ireland looking at some of its sites and then made our way to Belfast to find a hotel for the night. By the time we got there it was pretty much dark so you could see the flashing blue lights from quite a distance.

"Hmm, that's not good." I said to myself. I could see Steve trying to stop but the Police waved us on. We kept on getting waved on so ended up riding to the port, we bought some tickets to Stranraer and rode onto the ferry.

The crossing was just over two hours and I was looking forward to getting some sleep but with all the goings on there was no way I was going to get any. I ate some more food and went outside to watch to last of the light disappearing from the horizon.

By the time we reached Stranraer I was knackered. Steve wanted to ride all the way from Scotland to his home in Brighton but there was no way I was going to be able to do that without splatting myself over the windscreen of a passing lorry so we said our goodbyes.

I got on the A75 and then the M6 keeping my eyes peeled for a Welcome Break or Travelodge. By the time I found one it was approaching midnight and I was seriously running out of steam. It had started to rain and as I rode into the car park I almost dropped the bike. I parked up, spent twenty minutes taking my luggage off the bike and lugged it into the reception.

"One room for one weary traveller please." I noticed that I was so tired and cold that I was actually slurring my words. The lady looked at me with a face that read *'you're going to hate me forever'* and told me that they had no rooms whatsoever. I asked her if there was anywhere else I could stay "like a broom cupboard" but the only place she knew of was 135 miles south. She told me she would call ahead and reserve it for me.

With the room reserved I just had to cover the 135 miles and I'd have a nice bed for the night. With that light at the end of the tunnel I knew I could make it. I dragged my luggage out into the rain and strapped it all back onto my bike ready for the miserable ride.

As I left the carpark the rain really came down, I should have pulled over but there was no way I was going to stop. After twenty minutes my hands were numb, my groin was completely soaked and my visor was so fogged up that I may as well have been using *the force*.

Riding a bike at night in the rain is quite a weird experience. There is an element of being cocooned in your own little bubble. You're obviously outside but not completely, your crash helmet and leathers make you feel as if you're actually in your own small cockpit. I was thinking about how the other drivers would be looking at me saying *'poor sod'* when I felt the buzz of my tyres going over the rumple strips at the side of the road.

"Shit me!" I'd gone to sleep and wandered from the slow lane, across the middle and fast lanes to the rumple strips to the right of the fast lane! The bike and I did some serious wobbling but I managed to just about avoid smacking into the barrier. I got back into the slow lane and started singing to keep myself awake.

"I love the sun it shines on me, God made the Sun and God made me." This went on for some time but I was losing it so pulled over on the hard shoulder. I checked my odometer, I'd covered 35 miles, only another 100 to go.

I removed my crash helmet and jacket jogged up the hard shoulder and back to try to wake myself up. I started to feel a little better so got back on the bike and headed off.

"So, here I am on the motorway in the pissing rain talking to myself in a very loud voice trying to stay awake. I'm buzzing along at seventy-five miles per hour in the slow lane, yes Mr Georgiou, the slow lane, not the middle lane, or the fast lane, not even the grass in the middle, right in the middle of the slow lane. I'm turning my head to the side to allow the cold rain to enter my jacket and freeze my tits off. Yes, I did say freeze my tits off. I'm still in the slow lane and I'm awake and not dreaming. I see lights up ahead and will move over to the middle lane when the lights get closer so I can overtake him because I'm so awake."

I blabbered on like this for about twenty minutes but it was tiresome and I eventually quietened down and slipped back into my little cocoon. When I looked down to see how far I'd gone I realised that I'd slowed to about 25 mph. I pulled over, removed my helmet and jacket and did some pacing. When I checked the odometer I was astounded to find that I only had about fifteen miles to go!

I managed to wobble my way through the fifteen miles and finally pulled into the car park. It was surprisingly busy for 3:45 in the morning but I didn't care. I carefully removed my bags and made my way inside. There was a very unhappy man in front of me who was desperate for a room but the pretty receptionist was not going to budge one inch.

"I'm afraid I can't give you what I don't have Sir."

Good for her, I thought, sticking to her guns and not giving him my reservation. I liked her straight away. I thought about how much better the world would be if everyone was like her. Mr Unhappy stomped off into the rain.

"Hi, one of your offices 130 miles north called you and made a reservation for me, the name's Georgiou." She looked at her hands and sighed.

"Sorry love, we're full."

I told her about the reservation but she told me she couldn't give me what she didn't have. I dragged my bags to the edge of the room and slumped down on the floor. As my eyes closed I could feel my body shutting down. Three seconds to sleep, two seconds to sleep, one sec …

"If you don't leave I'll be forced to call the Police."

I opened my eyes, the receptionist now had a face like a slapped arse and was standing over me with a deadly serious look.

"No need for that" I said "They'll spot the accident on their cameras."

I lugged my body into a standing position, picked up my luggage and made my way outside. When I reached the bike I took off my wet tee-shirt and jumper and dug around in my luggage until I found what I was looking for; my favourite blue jumper that I've had since I was about twelve. I stood there in the cold strapping my luggage back onto the bike muttering obscenities about the hard-assed bitch receptionist from hell.

As I swung my leg over I lost my balance and dropped the bike. I didn't bother trying to pick it up, I knew it would be a futile exercise. I just stood there looking at the bike on its side feeling completely numb. Within ten seconds two men came over and helped me pick it up.

"You okay son?" I nodded slowly and did my best to smile "I'm just tired. They're full." I got on my bike and rode off.

I rode out of the services and back onto the motorway. I took the first slip road I came to and kept my eyes peeled for an area that I could sleep on. Bingo!

My penthouse for the night was a layby on a not so busy A road. The ground was far from flat but was reasonably dry. I unpacked my sleeping bag, put it inside my bivvy bag, climbed in, zipped everything up and went to sleep.

DAY FIVE

I woke to the sound of traffic, rain and wind. I attempted to roll over but it felt like someone was sitting on me. I fumbled around trying to find the zip for my bivvy bag but couldn't find it. Instead I just grabbed the top and pulled it apart. That was when all hell broke loose.

Floods of cold water came gushing into my sleeping bag soaking me from head to toe. I attempted to jump up but was still dressed in my motorbike leathers. I was also inside my heavy-weight army sleeping bag which was inside my bivvy bag which was now full of water. By the time I managed to get out I was soaking wet and freezing cold.

I was greeted by a horrible site. The wind was blowing the rain sideways, everywhere was covered in mud, my sleeping bag and bivvy were in a depression that was filled with muddy water, my boots were filled with water and my crash helmet was sitting upside down in a puddle.

My emotional state at this time was, shall we say, fragile. I decided that the last thing I needed to do was to have a tantrum. I would calmly pack up my stuff and ride home. I started with my sleeping bag. I tried just stuffing it into my pannier but it wouldn't fit, it needed to be rolled up tight. So, in the pouring rain in a muddy layby somewhere in northern England I carefully laid out my sleeping bag, knelt down at one end and did my level best to roll it up nice and tightly.

After a few minutes I had it rolled up but the bloody thing would still not fit into my pannier. I was getting more and more pissed off with every minute that passed. I threw it down on the ground and shook it out. This time I rolled it up as tight as was humanly possible. After a good five minutes of pushing and shoving I attempted to get it into the pannier but nope, it was not going in.

"FUCKING HELL!"

I threw the sleeping bag back in the puddle and jumped up and down on it as I shouted. My crash helmet got launched into the woods, my boots got kicked across the layby and I basically threw the most God almighty paddy you can imagine. After my tirade I just sat down in the mud, leant back against my bike and put my head in my hands.

I'm not sure how long I was there for but I was still shaking when a friendly face appeared next to me.

"You look like you need a coffee."

I looked up. He pointed over to a large articulated lorry that was parked in the layby on the other side of the road.

"It's got heating too." He said with a friendly smile.

I got up out of the mud and followed him to his truck. He laid his coat over the seat and I sat on that. It was so warm and comfortable and clean that I wondered what on Earth I'd done getting a bike. Why would a sane person do such a thing? He made me a strong coffee and offered me milk and sugar, I shook my head as I took the coffee.

"What I could really do with though is a cigarette."

He smiled and told me to follow him. We went round the back of his truck, he opened the doors and we climbed in. His entire lorry was full of boxes of cigarettes! He gave me two packs of Marlboro Lights and a lighter. I said thank you and went back to the bike.

I stood there next to my bike with my pack of Marlboro Lights. I removed the cellophane and opened the top. The silver paper was quickly removed as I raised the pack to my nose. I smelt the contents.

"Tobacco, I've missed you." I said out loud. There should have been a little voice saying
"What the FUCK are you doing!" but there wasn't. There was only me and a Marlboro Light. I removed a cigarette from the packet and lit the end. The smoke was inhaled in a deep lung full of nastiness. It felt wonderful. The red anger, the hot frustration, the need to lash out all became secondary to the immense satisfaction of *the present*. The world became a better place and that was okay with me.

With my mind at ease I was able to think straight. I removed all the clothing from my waterproof duffle bag and placed it into one of my panniers. This allowed me to stuff my sopping sleeping bag into the duffle. I reminded myself that brains were better than brawn. Problem solved. Putting my sodden boots on was not a nice experience but I didn't care. There was no point in using carrier bags to keep my feet dry as my socks were completely soaked too.

My crash helmet was soaking wet and full of dirt. I wiped out as much as I could then stuck it on my head. As I pushed my head in I compressed the saturated padding which caused to cold water to run down my back. I was ready to ride.

The first ten miles were pretty miserable but soon enough the clouds got higher and allowed the sun through. The warm sun reminded me that there was more to life than just mud, misery and cold water. As I continued south it warmed up considerably and when I came across a sign that gave me an option of Wales I thought about it for a second, then took the slip road.

Snowdonia is one of my favourite places and it was (kind of) on my way home. What's one more night anyway? As I left the vicinity of Manchester the traffic almost disappeared and the roads improved considerably. Within a couple of hours of my dismal start to the day I was swooping around the meandering roads of North Wales with a grin from ear to ear. As I made my way through the windy roads I thought about motorbikes and how they can be hard work but can also offer the very best of times. The phrase that came to mind was *work hard, play hard*. I know that's not quite right but you get the point.

My excitement rose in line with the altitude as I rode into Snowdonia. Mountains have always held a special place in my heart and every time I visit Snowdonia is like the first.
I spent my afternoon enjoying the combination of my bike, winding roads and the beautiful Welsh countryside. I stopped at a small shop and bought some provisions for my evening meal. I took my time and made sure I got all the ingredients I needed and a nice bottle of red wine. Happy that I was armed with enough to cook myself a culinary masterpiece (rather than my normal *coronary fry-up*) I made my way back to a place I'd found earlier that

looked like a camping possibility.

The layby where I chose to camp wasn't your typical beauty spot but it had a fantastic view and it was all mine. I grabbed my tent and picked a spot. As I walked over to where I was planning to pitch up I watched as a few small stones broke free from a huge boulder above me and made their way down to my pitch. The gigantic boulder stayed put but after the earlier tree incident I decided to find another spot to camp.

With my tent back on the bike I jumped aboard and rode towards Betws-y-Coed. On the way I spotted a sign with a tent so decided to follow it. I'm not sure if I went wrong or if the camp site had shut down but either way I couldn't find it. Instead, I found a small piece of rough ground with a shallow river at one end and no houses anywhere to be seen. I'd found my camping spot for the night.

I carefully rode to the river and stopped the bike. I got off and stood there with the contentment of knowing I had a wonderful evening ahead of me. Instead of cracking on with tent and food preparation I decided to get in the river and have an all over wash. After looking around I stripped my clothes off and got in. The water was so cold that should someone have been standing there watching they would not have been able to see anything anyway, if you know what I mean?!

I managed to completely and thoroughly wash every smelly bit of my body inside of about 90 seconds and promptly got out. As I stood there at the side of the river stark bollock naked I looked up and saw a young couple in walking gear not fifty feet away. I had two choices, get back in the freezing river and hide or make a run for it and hope I reached my towel before they looked in my direction.

"What the hell." I grabbed my goolies and ran towards the bike. Once I reached the bike I frantically unpacked until I found my towel. As I wrapped myself up the walkers looked over and waved. I waved back but busied myself in the hope they got the message. Drying ones testicles is not a spectator sport after all. The walkers walked on.

Once dry and in fresh clothes I was keen to get everything set up for my perfect evening. Before even thinking about food or wine I needed to get my tent up. Whilst I unpacked everything off the bike I thought about the difference between my morning and my evening. This whole trip had been about extremes, some good and some completely crap. I was hoping all the crap bits were behind me.

As I stood there admiring the fact that I was all set up and ready to cook a tractor slowed down and turned into the field I was in. The equipment hanging off the rear end said business but the driver was smiling from ear to ear. He drove over the field and stopped next to my bike. I looked up thanking God that he hadn't turned up twenty minutes earlier.

"Perfect place for camping eh?" The tractor driver said.
"It's beautiful. I followed signs and got a bit lost. Am I okay here?" I said with my fingers crossed.

It turned out that he was the owner/farmer and he was just doing the rounds. He could come back tomorrow and do this field. What a lovely chap!

With permission granted and all my wet clothes and sleeping bag hanging over the bike I felt I could finally relax. I sat on the grass and enjoyed a small glass of Merlot as I watched nature continue around me. The beautiful sound of trickling water, the leaves rustling in the light breeze and bird song all culminated in a moment of pure contentment that I will remember for a long time.

Over the next hour I carefully concocted my culinary masterpiece; a most delicious chilli con carne. In between each check I read my book and drank my wine. When I think of motorbike travelling this is exactly the image I conjure up in my head; a beautiful field next to a stream, sunshine, birds signing, butterflies flitting over the grassy meadow, a nice wine and the aroma of cooked food. These times do happen but they're not as regular an occurrence as the completely miserable times. Perhaps it's their rarity that makes them all the more wonderful. I thought back to the morning when I opened up my sleeping bag and laughed to myself. Is variety not the spice of life?

DAY SIX – THE RIDE HOME

After such a delightful evening I half expected the morning after to be full of rain, mud and misery but that couldn't have been further from the truth. I unzipped the tent and was presented with the most glorious of mornings. The sun was shining, the birds were singing and the temperature was a good 20 degrees.

I put some water on to boil and went over to the river for a wash. On my return I made myself a coffee, lit up a cigarette and sat there absorbed in the beauty of the moment.

Soon enough it was time to leave so everything was packed up and readied for my trip home. As I rode out of the field I stopped and looked back; what a wonderful place. I engaged first gear, leant the bike over slightly, released the clutch and started the final leg of my trip.

The last day's miles were easy ones that seemed to zip past effortlessly. The traffic was light, the end was in sight and the fabulous weather accompanied me all the way to my front door. As I bumbled onwards getting ever closer to home I thought about the highs and lows of the trip and came to the conclusion that the wonder of travelling by motorbike is the extremes, not just the good but the bad too. It's the rawness of actually being in the film, not just sitting on the sofa watching it.

========= THE END =========

EPILOGUE

I don't think it would be pushing the boundaries of truth to say that getting a motorbike, and obviously a license, literally changed my life for the better. I've always had an adventurous streak but it was never really realized until I got a motorbike.

Travelling by motorbike can be incredibly hard work; however, the freedom and feelings of being in touch with the places you ride through all come together to make it feel worthwhile. And, when those rare moments of pure beauty happen, being on a motorbike is the cherry on top.

Whether knee deep in mud and excrement, or lost in a beauty spot and deep in contentment, I know I've found my means, not only of transport, but of adventure too.

ABOUT THE AUTHOR

Richard lives in a small village in the East Sussex countryside with his wife Flowie, Newfoundland dog Nelly and their two cats Frodo and Kiri. He came to biking rather late in life after watching an episode of Long Way Down.

A career change from computer programming to running his own company supplying medical products to the general public allowed a freedom that Richard used to indulge in his two passions; motorbikes and writing.

Long may it last.

If you enjoyed this and want to read about my month long, ten thousand mile, solo trip to the Sahara desert you can purchase "One Man on a Bike" from here:
www.onemanonabike.com